HOW TO DRAW & PAINT
PORTRAITS

CONTENTS

Portrait

IN SPITE OF the old adage that the face reflects the soul, the foibles, failings, and weaknesses of man are not usually shown openly in the portrait. The reason for this, of course, is that the sitter, or whoever commissions the portrait, invariably wishes to present his or her best appearances, as the actor will insist on the camera catching his 'good side'. In spite of this, the true portrait artist – as opposed to the photocopyist – will often show depths of character and shades of cunning or synthetic emotions better than any other means of making a likeness of the sitter.

Likeness is an indispensable part of portraiture, but by no means the whole story: qualities of color can aid the feeling of the spirit of the sitter; intelligent composition can render frailty or pompous bulk.

The self portrait

Because the history of portraiture is studded with so many fine gems, to find one's own language, to avoid the pitfalls of sentimentality and deadness, is often difficult. Many artists use the self portrait as a way to guarantee a consistent model and to allow a subject for experiment, both with descriptions of form and the way

of approaching problems.

Throughout the centuries man has ventured to create images of himself, often using the self portrait as a background figure or as a character in animation. The self portrait as an art form, in its own right, was taken to very high levels of achievement by Rembrandt, Van Gogh, and Cézanne, all of whom used it to discover their personal means of picture making. It remains an extremely useful way to gain knowledge and will give aspiring portraitists valuable opportunities to experiment and risk making mistakes.

The support

When setting out to make a portrait, it is important to consider the shape of the support upon which the picture will be made. A subject painted full length does not necessarily demand a tall, thin canvas for it may be that the figure will be better seen or the character better expressed by putting it alongside other objects. This is a way to increase interest in the composition; the tendency to place the sitter in the middle of the picture and fill in the background often creates boring images. A study of the portrait paintings of old and modern masters from this point of view will reveal a good

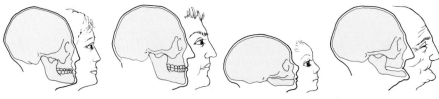

Bone structure. Left: to right: The female skull is smaller than the male with less pronounced forehead and chin. The male skull has a strong jawline and forehead. The child's head is largely undeveloped. With age, bone deteriorates.

Expressions. Expression is created by the tensing and relaxing of muscles. Left: A worried expression is altered by an overhead light source. Right: The smile creates a turning upward of all features, most notably the eyes and forehead; the frown causes the opposite.

4

Rembrandt van Rijn, 'Self Portrait'. Rembrandt's series of self portraits are renowned for their technical skill and ability to depict a sombre and intense atmosphere.

A successful portrait can be achieved with either a quick, informal sketch, or an elaborate oil painting. <u>Left:</u> In this pencil sketch by <u>Augustus John</u>, we see how the skilled handling of tone and line capture the mood and personality of the sitter. <u>Above:</u> The 'Laughing Cavalier' by <u>Franz Hals,</u> although elaborate in the use of detail and ornamentation is nonetheless successful in portraying the personality of the sitter.

Henri Matisse, 'Portrait of Derain'. The Fauve group exploited the use of pure, broken color to create dramatic pictures.

deal of the mechanics of picture construction.

Color

Color will always be a challenge to the portraitist. At first sight it would appear that a portrait would be dominated by flesh tones. This, though, is not always the case as witnessed in the portraits by Derain, Matisse, and the candle-lit flesh tints of a de la Tour. By deciding upon a color idea – that is, a scheme of color that both harmonizes and reflects the feelings one has towards the subject – the picture will get off to a good start. An elegant lady with jewellery and silks will need a different color idea than that used in painting a baby or the noble head of an old man. Flesh itself varies in color a great deal from the pink blush in a Fragonard (1732–1806) to the dry tints in a Wyeth, or the modulated tones in a Franz Hals (1585–1666).

To experiment with the mixtures that might result in descriptive flesh tones is essential, and to use a mixture of techniques desirable. Limited palettes for flesh painting have always proved most successful. A good, general palette that will mix in several ways would consist of yellow ochre, light red, terre verte, cobalt blue, and flake white. By mixing the yellow and red with perhaps a touch of terre verte or blue, a good general tint will be achieved. By using this limited palette discoveries will be made as to how red and blue, or blue and green, or any other multi-mixtures, will correspond to the colors seen.

Shadows should be carefully analysed so that when painted in they are never simply a darkened version of the general color in the lighter areas; each each shadow has its own color and

tone. The shadows in the face and hands or any other flesh areas will be affected by external colors being reflected into them. Thus, the shadow on a nose might well have a green cast to the color whereas the darker, warmer tones beneath the eyebrows might contain a purplish-brown. By experimenting with both the 'reflected' shadow colors and the local, lighter colors, one will discover the value of understanding and using the various color theories.

Drawing media

The pencil has long been regarded as excellent for portrait drawing. Ingres was an artist who demonstrated consummate skills in this medium, able at once to describe character, clothing, and often bring the whole picture into context with the briefest description of background. As an alternative to this, the hatching method has much to commend it. By using a hard pencil to sketch in the basic shapes and proportions, and using progressively softer leads to mass in the shadows and tones and describe details, control can be sustained throughout the drawing process.

With pen and ink, using diluted ink and gradually strenthening the density of tones to build up the face and costume is a useful method of tackling portraits. Charles Keene, a contemporary artist, makes use of a wide range of marks with great subtlety, whereas Phil May, another 20th century artist, used the pen line in a more direct, linear way, involving a thrilling calligraphic line. This means requires practice and experience. Try using solid areas of ink to suggest 'color' as in hair mass or boots, contrasted with a smooth, flowing line.

Positioning. Placement of the figure is important in all picture making. Here the figure has been dropped below the center-line bringing the observer's eye into the subject.

Classic view. The three-quarter view is the traditional pose for portraiture. This has been used extensively because it incorporates as much of the full face and profile of a figure as possible

The profile. The profile was more common in the past than today. It can be a difficult pose to capture and care is required to avoid flatness. It is useful to include some of the figure as well.

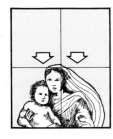

Direction. This too is a very important factor in all painting and drawing. Notice how the downward glance of the figure tends to lead the observer's eye downward as well.

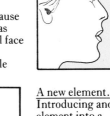

Background. The background of a portrait can add a great deal to what the artist is attempting to say about the sitter.

A new element. Introducing another element into a portrait – in this case the sitter's hand – can often enliven a picture. Note how the hand supports the head giving a feeling of stability.

Oil

IN ART HISTORICAL terms, the technique of working on a stark, white canvas is a recent development made popular by the Impressionists of the last century. Before that time it was customary to work on a colored ground, made either by mixing pigment into the priming coat or laying a thin wash of color over a white base. The purpose of this was to establish a middle tone over which to work with light and dark colors and to give the image a warm or cool cast.

The red priming used in this painting is a powerful color which radically affects the whole character of the painting. The forms are constructed with a variety of greys; those which tend toward blue or green are emphasized on the strong red ground, and pink and yellow flesh tones pick up the warm glow of red which breaks through. Although the palette is limited, the relationships of the colors are vibrant and active. You will need to pay close attention to both the subject and the painting to achieve a lively but controlled result.

Use thick, dry paint and keep the brushwork loose and open so the red is seen through the broken color. Stiff bristle brushes are effective for this if handled lightly and vigorously. Keep the paint dry, adding only a small amount of turpentine, or the colors will flood the surface and deaden as they dry out.

Materials

Surface
Canvas primed with red oil-based primer

Size
30in × 26in (75cm × 65cm)

Tools
Nos 3, 6, flat bristle brushes
Palette

Colors
Black	Foundation white
Chrome yellow	Oxide of chromium
Cobalt blue	Permanent rose

Medium
Turpentine

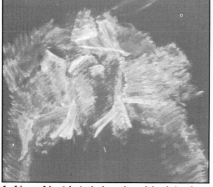

1. Use a No 6 bristle brush to block in the basic shape of the figure in white. With a No 3 brush, sketch in the outline and lay areas of light tone.

2. Mix two tones of grey from cobalt blue, black and white. Work over the whole canvas in thin patches of color.

3. Develop the dark tones around the hat, shoulders and neck. Add a little yellow to the greys and block in the tones behind the head and in the hat.

4. Work into the face and neck with a light greenish-grey, roughly mapping out the features. Build up the structure of the image, with detail in the hat and collar.

5. Develop the color in the face using cool blue-grey contrasted with a warm flesh tone mixed from yellow, rose, and white. Indicate features with light marks.

6. Draw into the features with dark red, black and white. Block in light tones on the shirt with solid grey and white.

7. Work over the whole image with thick paint developing the tonal structure with warm greys in the foreground and light grey-green in the background.

8. Work over the figure with a No 3 brush, dabbing in color to refine details and add definition to the features.

Finished picture · outlining in white · scratching back

By completion of the painting,(<u>above</u>) the strong red underpainting is almost completely obscured, yet its subtle influence can be seen in the warm cast of the image.

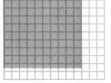

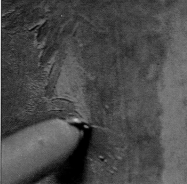

Using the end of the brush, the artist is here scratching back through the wet paint layer to allow the underpainting to break through to the surface.

Using undiluted white paint, the artist roughs in the general composition and figure outlines over the dry red underpainting.

ONE OF THE most interesting aspects of this painting is how few colors were used to effectively render the subject and its environment. The artist has relied only upon tones of burnt umber, burnt sienna, ochre, and white for almost the entire painting. This stresses the wisdom of the artist familiarizing himself with the many color mixes that can be attained from using a limited palette. The knowledge gained from working in this way is greater than using a variety of colors as the same principles apply to using many colors as to using a few. Thus the knowledge and experienced gained by using a limited palette can later be used with any number of colors.

The strength of the picture comes not only from the simplicity of the palette, but from the composition as well. This is – as any successful composition should be – not obvious, but has the subtle effect of directing the viewer's attention where the artist intends it to go. The artist intentionally left a great deal of space around the figure. Coupled with the pale strip down the right hand side and the off-centre placement of the subject, the viewer's eyes are drawn directly into the figure.

Materials

Surface
Primed cotton duck

Size
23in × 30in (57cm × 75cm)

Tools
HB pencil
Nos 2 and 4 flat bristle brushes
No 5 sable round watercolor brush
1½in (3.75cm) housepainting brush
Fixative
Palette

Colors

Black	Raw sienna
Burnt sienna	Scarlet lake
Burnt umber	White
Cobalt blue	Yellow ochre

Medium
Turpentine

1 Begin to block in shadow areas in burnt and raw sienna with a No 5 sable brush. Add white to the sienna and work into the eye area in detail with a No 2 brush.

2 Continue to block in the shadows of the face with a thinned mixture of burnt umber and white.

3. Continue to block in highlight areas with white and ochre. Add a touch of scarlet lake to warm the flesh tones.

4. Put in mouth details with the No 2 brush and scarlet lake, yellow ochre and white. Add touches of highlight in the ear. Blend again with a clean, large brush.

5. Begin to lay in the pattern of the jacket with loose strokes of burnt umber with a No 4 brush. Rough in the outline of the arm and scrub in the shadow area.

6. Next block in lighter jacket areas in yellow ochre. With a 1½in (3.75cm) housepainting brush, blend tones together. *(continued overleaf)*

Initial drawing · modelling face · blending highlights

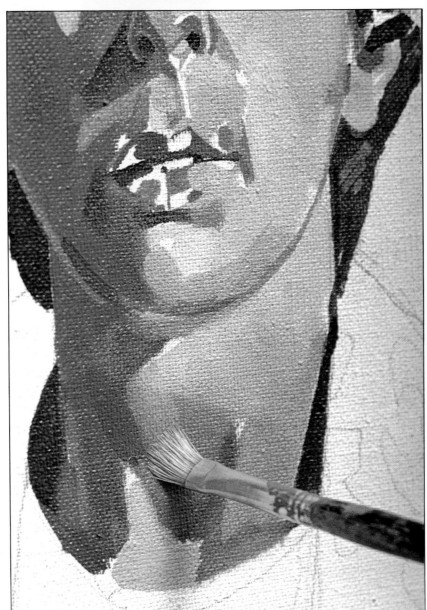

The figure is first drawn in with light pencil strokes (<u>top</u>) including as much detail as possible. Using a small sable brush and warm and cool flesh tones, the artist begins to model the face of the figure (<u>above</u>) working from one point outwards. Moving downwards, larger areas of highlights are blocked in and then blended into surrounding areas with a dry, clean brush (<u>right</u>).

Coat pattern · working inside and outside the figure

Coat pattern · working inside and outside the figure

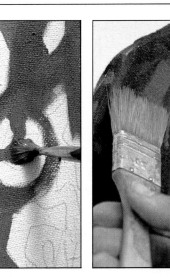

To create the pattern of the coat, the artist first describes the lighter pattern and fills in the white areas with a darker tone. Then, with a clean, dry decorators' brush, the colors are blended together with a feathering motion, the brush just lightly touching the surface.

Working outside the figure (above), the background is roughed in with the decorators' brush. A clean edge between background and figure is obtained by using a smaller brush and background color. Moving into the figure (left), the shirt is carefully described in tones of grey and white.

7. Continue to define the pattern in burnt umber and fill in with yellow ochre. Darken shadow area around collar. Block in the right side with burnt sienna.

9. With a No 4 brush and grey paint, block in the shirt. With burnt sienna, raw umber, and the housepainting brush, cover the background area.

11 Work back into the right side of the jacket with gold ochre, scrubbing in highlight areas.

8. Continue to put in the pattern in burnt umber and yellow ochre. Mix scarlet lake and yellow ochre for the highlight areas. Rough in the shirt shadow in grey.

10. Smooth out the background with the housepainting brush and a lighter brown made from burnt umber and white.

12. Block in the pattern with the no 4 brush and burnt umber.

THE PORTRAIT shown was executed quickly. However, because a very rich mixture of paint and oil medium was used, the painting had to be allowed to dry thoroughly between stages to avoid muddying the colors and surface.

The artist was chiefly concerned with the fine details of the painting – for example the model's features – until the final steps. In these last few steps broad, general areas of the figure were tightened up and the final detailed touches – those which turned the work from a figure painting into a portrait – were put into the painting.

The subject was never treated as a series of parts – face, torso, legs and arms – but was always considered as a complete unit throughout the painting process. Thus, if the artist applied a highlight in the face, he might very well use this same color in the dress and hands. This method of painting unifies the image by the use of similar colors placed throughout the figure. As well, it prevents the artist from seeing the subject as a number of parts, but as a whole unit in which every area – no matter how small – directly affects every other area.

Materials

Surface
Prepared canvas board

Size
14in × 18in (35cm × 45cm)

Tools
No 6 flat bristle brush
No 4 sable round brush
Palette

Colors
Alizarin crimson   Cobalt blue
Black   Terre verte
Burnt umber   White
Cadmium red light   Yellow ochre

Mediums
Turpentine
Linseed oil

Blending with fingers · describing hands

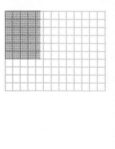

The artist has purposely avoided using small areas of detail except in the face of the model. Details are not always needed to accurately and effectively render a subject, as seen in the sitter's hands.

1. With red, yellow ochre, and a mixture of blue and alizarin crimson, block in the general color areas of the figure in a thinnish wash with a No 6 brush.

2. Add white to these colors and block in the lighter areas of the figure with long strokes. Using the color of the skirt highlight, put in the strip on the left side.

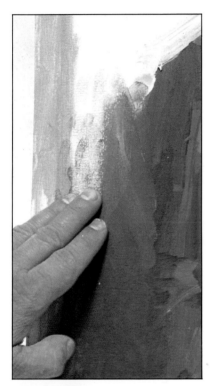

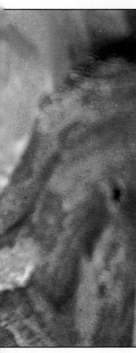

Rather than using a brush or rag, the artist is here using his fingers to blend the figure's shoulder into the background. Blending with the fingers produces a subtle, smudged effect unobtainable by other means.

3. Block in the hair with burnt umber and a No 4 sable brush. Mix terre verte, white, and linseed oil and loosely put in general facial features. Blend left side of coat.

4. Using cobalt blue and black, work into the dark shadow areas of the skirt. With the same tone, loosely block in shadows on the left side of the shirt.

5. Mix white, terre verte, and a small amount of cobalt blue and block in grey area to left. Work into the left side of the face with terre verte and white.

6. Put in scarf details in blue and white. mix grey tone and put in brick details behind figure. Touch in dark details of face and skirt highlights.

WHILE A SUCCESSFUL portrait is never an easy thing to achieve, there are certain techniques which will facilitate the process.

In terms of capturing a likeness, the key to a successful portrait is to make sure that the first basic step – the preliminary drawing – is as accurate as possible. If the features are not correctly positioned and described at the outset, there is little chance of success and the artist will find himself repeatedly laying down paint, scraping it off, and reworking in an attempt to correct the original drawing.

Once the preliminary work is as accurate as possible, do not be over-concerned with details. The most important thing at this stage is to check and recheck the positioning of the features while you work. A face is not made up of a series of individual parts; always judge distance and relative size by comparing one feature to another.

If you work in thin rather than thick washes of color, there is less danger of building up the paint surface too quickly. It is easier to correct and revise thin layers of paint then thick. Work in light-dark and warm-cool tones and keep the palette as simple as possible. The artist here used a minimum of colors, with the addition of white, to successfully capture the subject of the portrait.

Materials

Surface
Prepared canvas board

Size
9in × 10in (22.5cm × 25cm)

Tools
No 6 flat bristle brush
No 4 round sable brush
Palette

Colors
Burnt sienna
Burnt umber
Cadmium red deep
Gold ochre
White

Mediums
Turpentine
Linseed oil

1. With a No 4 sable brush and a wash of turpentine and burnt umber, block in outlines, facial features and the start of the background.

2. With a No 6 bristle brush, block in the hair in gold ochre and background in thinned umber. Use burnt sienna and white for the face tones.

3. Mix a deeper shade of burnt umber and paint over background. Work into the hair. With burnt sienna and white put in shadow areas on right.

4. Put in lips with cadmium red and white mixture. Put in touches of dark shadow with the sable brush and burnt umber.

5. With pure cadmium red, paint in the necklace. Mix warmish tones of burnt sienna, red and white and work over the face, blending in the paint.

6. With a mixture of burnt umber and white, re-define the facial planes with even strokes. Mix white, cadmium green and yellow ochre and cover in the background.

Hair shadows

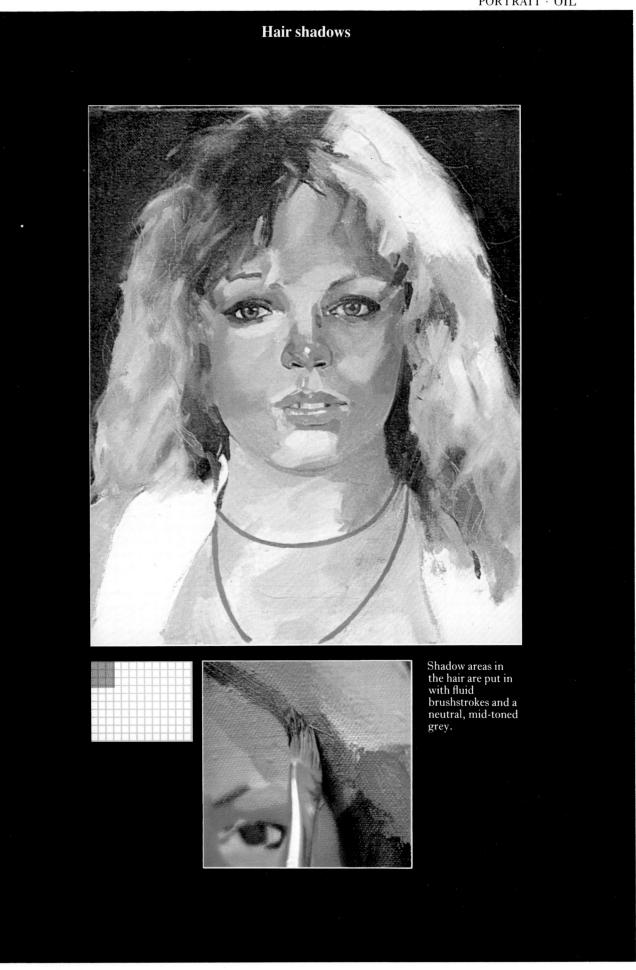

Shadow areas in the hair are put in with fluid brushstrokes and a neutral, mid-toned grey.

Hair shadows

THE TECHNIQUES USED for this portrait demonstrate an oil painting method which is essentially direct and spontaneous both in the drawing and application of color. As the painting was completed in only two sittings, the paint had no time to dry. For this reason the artist would occasionally blot the painting surface with a rag or sheet of paper to lift excess moisture.

A color photograph rather than live subject was used for the painting, but the information supplied was used only for the groundwork of the painting and the end result is not a straightforward copy. Photographs tend to flatten subtleties of tone and color, so it is necessary to add to the image by strengthening or even exaggerating certain elements. In this example, the background color and patterns in the clothes were altered as the painting progressed.

Work rapidly with stiff bristle brushes to block in the overall impression of the image, using the brushmarks to indicate the structure and texture of the forms. Small sable brushes are more suitable for adding fine points of detail. Experiment with colour mixes on a separate piece of paper or board to find the right tones for subtle flesh colours and shadows.

Materials

Surface
Primed hardboard

Size
12in × 18in (30cm × 45cm)

Tools
No 3 flat bristle brush
No 5 sable round brush
Newspaper
Palette

Colors
Alizarin crimson	Ultramarine blue
Black	Vermilion
Cadmium yellow	Van Dyke brown
Chrome oxide	White
Cobalt blue	Yellow ochre

Mediums
Turpentine
Linseed oil

Face shadows · eye details · blotting

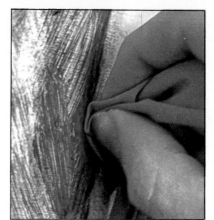

While the paint is still wet, the artist cleans up the facial area where background color has run over with a small piece of rag and turpentine.

If the paint surface becomes too wet to work on, a piece of newspaper or absorbent towelling can be laid over it, lightly pressed, and lifted off. Be sure not to press too hard or to move the paper on the surface.

With a small brush and a middle flesh tone, the artist begins to work into the details of the eye over the dry underpainting. Note how the underpainting shows through the paint.

1. Use brown and blue to make a neutral color and outline the basic shape of the face and features with a No 3 bristle brush.

2. Start to define warm and cool color areas with flesh tones, dark yellow and brown. Strengthen the background color and cover the entire background area.

3. Spread the paint in the background and lighten highlight areas with a dry rag. Use dark colors and flesh tones in the face, using the No 3 bristle brush.

4. Paint shadows on the head and neck with dark red and work over the hair and beard with greenish-brown.

5. Build up shadows and highlights in the face and hair using small dabbing strokes to blend the colors. Darken the left side of the background.

6. Blot off the excess paint from the whole surface with a sheet of newspaper. Applying the paint more thickly, build up the dark tones.

7. Use a No 5 sable to apply highlights of light yellow and pink. Paint the jacket with a thick layer of light color.

8. Work over the whole image, blending the colors and redefining the forms. Give the shadows a slightly cooler cast with thin overlays of yellow ochre and brown.

9. Make a thin glaze of red paint, using an oil medium, and work over the flesh tones. Strengthen the highlights with thick dabs of white paint. *(continued overleaf)*

Finished picture · shadows and highlights

As a final step, the artist decided to put a scarf around the man's neck (left).

This provides an interesting contrast to the face and liveliness of the image.

With a fine sable brush, the artist develops the shadow and highlight areas around the eye.

Small touches of highlight and shadow are put in with a small brush in the final stages of the painting. Here the artist defines the model's ear.

10. Lighten the color of the background, at the same time correcting the outlines.

11. Alter the tone of the whole background area, leaving a darker shadow at one side of the face.

12. Using the background color as a guide, make adjustments to the tone and color over the entire image, blending the paint with light strokes of the brush.

PAINTING A PORTRAIT in profile, as opposed to the traditional full-faced approach, can yield interesting results. When working in this way, however, there is a danger of producing a flat and predictable picture. A bare profile against a plain background can easily become simplistic and uninteresting to look at.

In this painting, the artist has avoided this in two ways. The face has been modelled with a textural and tonal complexity which overrides the simplicity of its shape and position on the canvas. The details of the hair, being the only part of the picture to incorporate fine lines of color, serve to bring the observer's eyes into the face. Curving downward and to the right, these details bring the eyes repeatedly into the subject area.

The artist has also exploited the dark blue background to heighten the lighter, warmer tones of the face and set off the profile in sharp contrast. The sitter appears to be cast in a strong, direct light, the source of which is unknown, and therefore the painting becomes more interesting to the viewer.

Materials

Surface
Prepared canvas board

Size
12in × 15in (30cm × 37.5cm)

Tools
Nos 2 and 4 flat bristle brushes
Palette
Palette knife

Colors

Black	Scarlet lake
Burnt sienna	Ultramarine
Burnt umber	White
Cadmium red medium	Yellow ochre

Mediums
Turpentine
Linseed oil

1. With a thin wash of turpentine and burnt umber, block in the shadow areas in hair and background. With a No 2 brush, establish facial features.

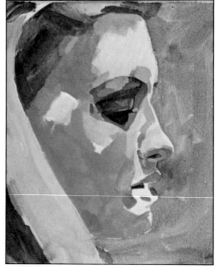

2. With a No 4 brush, mix a loose wash of cadmium red, umber and white and block in the red tones of the face. With yellow ochre and white, define highlight areas.

3. Mix black, white and a touch of burnt umber and put in the shadows around the eyes with the No 2 brush.

Finished picture

A profile can produce a strong, vibrant portrait as seen in the finished painting. Care must be taken to balance the bold outline of the profile with the background.

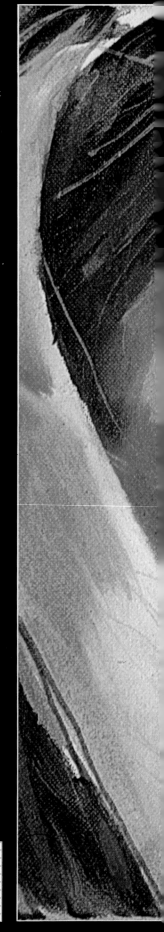

4. With white and a small amount of red, blend in warm highlights on cheek bones, forehead, and nose. Lay down color and blend with a clean, dry brush.

5. Mix umber and white and, with a No 4 brush, model in shadow areas of the chin, blending the edges into the previous layer.

6. Mix a wash of blue and black and, with a large brush, cover background area. With a small brush and white and yellow ochre, put in hair details.

Acrylic

PAINTING A portrait makes demands on the power of visual observation above and beyond those used in everyday contact. In creating a likeness, observation must be disciplined and critical. Every feature of the head and face must be carefully analysed in terms of color, shape, and tone in order to understand the relationships existing between them. Because the character of the image is dependent upon this detailed analysis, small adjustments at any stage of the painting can make all the difference between success and failure.

The nature of acrylic paints may help to overcome some of the problems of portrait painting. The basic form can be built up quickly with thin layers of paint which dry almost immediately. Fine details can then be painted over this mixture with no danger of the layers mixing and making the colors muddy. The shapes tend to be more distinct than in oil paint, which remains wet for a long period. Acrylic colors are vivid and opaque, so light and dark tones can be overlaid and mistakes covered completely.

Materials

Surface
Primed and stretched cotton duck

Size
18in × 20in (45cm × 50cm)

Tools
No 6 flat bristle brush
No 4 sable round brush
Palette
Stencil for making small dots

Colors

Black	Cobalt blue
Burnt sienna	Vermilion
Burnt umber	White
Cadmium yellow	Yellow ochre

Medium
Water

1. Working with black, white, vermilion and burnt sienna and a No 6 brush, block in an overall impression of the figure.

2. Lay in the light flesh tones of the face. Put a blue cast into the shadows with cobalt and grey, drawing small, precise shapes with the brush.

3. Add touches of vivid colour to the face by using rich reds and browns to define the mouth and lighten flesh tones with pale pinks and yellows.

4 Lay in the background colour with a No 6 brush and apply a thin wash of black. Adjust the contours of the figure with a smaller brush

5. Start to paint the pattern details on the dress using vivid colors. Draw the tiny shapes with the point of a brush, keeping the color thick and opaque.

6. Use a stencil to apply small pattern areas. Angle the dots to describe the directions of the form. Combine this with larger shapes painted by hand.

Stencilling in details

Using a stencil, the artist blocks in dots of yellow over the dry paint surface. These dots are then modified by further applications of color to vary their shape and size.

THE STYLE AND character of a person is expressed not only by the face, but also by clothes, posture, and the environment in which they live and work. A full-length portrait, will catch the viewer's attention if it include all of these aspects of the subject's individuality. A portrait should try to capture the mood of the sitter; for example, whether he or she is relaxed and confident, or presenting a formal, calculated pose. Such aspects should all be taken into consideration by all artists and will, to a large extent, determine the techniques chosen by them.

Here the artist has used acrylic paints on paper rather than canvas to make a quick, but detailed, study. This does not mean any special techniques or methods were used, but as the finished work is more easy to damage than one on canvas or board, it should be protected by glass.

A photograph was used for reference. This does away with the necessity of long, tiring sittings for the model but, since the range of information given by a photograph is limited, the artist therefore must be confident and inventive in his handling of the subject and the medium.

The colors of the painting are muted but warm and glowing. Areas of neutral brown are enlivened with touches of green and dark red in the shadows. The effect of bright, artificial lighting is enhanced by a strong cast of yellow in the highlights.

Materials

Surface
Stretched cartridge paper

Size
14.5in × 21in (36cm × 52.5cm)

Tools
No 6 sable round brush
No 5 flat bristle brush
Palette

Colors
Black   Pthalo crimson
Burnt sienna   Ultramarine blue
Burnt umber   Vermilion
Cadmium orange   White
Cadmium yellow   Yellow ochre

Medium
Water

1. Block in the basic image in thin color washes with a No 6 brush.

2. Work over the whole surface and intensify the tones with washes of black, brown and blue. Lay in solid blocks of color with a No 5 bristle brush.

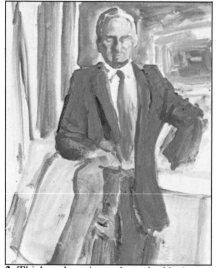

3. Thicken the paint and use the No 6 brush to lay in light flesh tones and blue-grey shadows. Work over the suit with grey and ultramarine.

4. Strengthen the background colour and block in the shape of the chair with yellow ochre and burnt sienna. Show folds in the suit with blue and grey draw tie pattern.

5. Work up the details of face and hands with strong contrasts of light and dark flesh tones.

6. Move across the painting laying small dabs of thick color to redefine details and add strong white highlights. Lighten the tones in the background.

Developing shadows · using the brushstroke

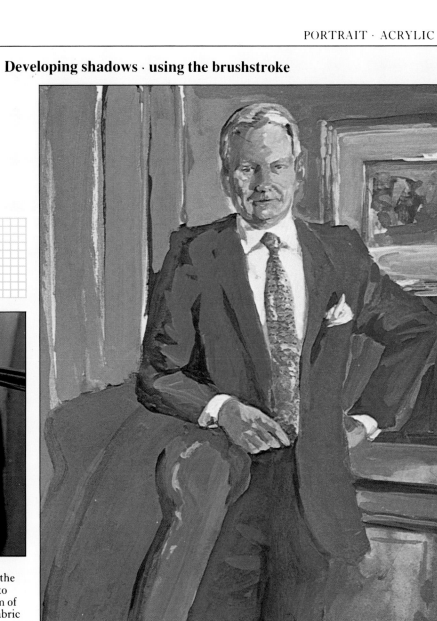

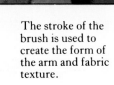

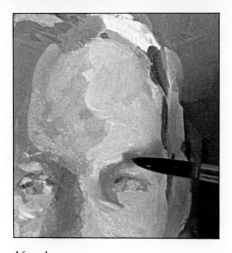

The stroke of the brush is used to create the form of the arm and fabric texture.

After the predominant flesh tones have been established, the artist develops subtle shadow areas with a warm, light brown.

THE CHIEF GOAL of the portrait artist to capture a likeness of the sitter, but the problems and pleasures of controlling the paint and developing color and texture also add another dimension to the challenge. Unlike a photograph, which duplicates almost exactly what the lens of the camera sees, the portraitist has the freedom to create not only a likeness, but an interesting painting as well.

A layered technique has been used here to keep the surface active and develop a wide tonal range. The dry-brush technique was used, which involves laying dry, broken color across the canvas weave by spreading the bristles of the brush. An alternative is to apply thin glazes of color, made more transparent by the addition of a glazing medium. By using these techniques, the colors and tones are successively modified to build up the form of the head. Thick dabs of opaque paint are overlaid to emphasize dark tones and vivid highlights.

The basic structure and proportions of the image are freely reworked throughout the process. There is no need to cover up all corrections and alterations; stray lines and patches of unexpected color may enliven the painting and give weight to the overall structure.

Materials

Surface
Prepared canvas board

Size
16in × 14in (40cm × 50cm)

Tools
No 5 flat bristle brushes
No 8 round sable brush
Palette

Colors
Black	Pthalo crimson
Burnt sienna	Prussian blue
Cadmium red light	Violet
Cadmium yellow	Yellow ochre

Quick-drying acrylics allow the artist to alter and correct his painting without interrupting the painting process. Here the artist is moving the entire face of the subject over by blocking in new highlight areas.

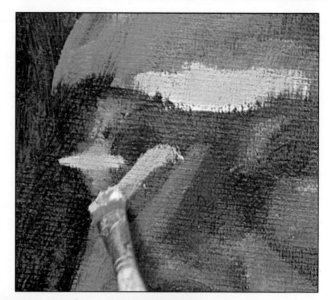

Shadow areas around the eyes are described with thick, opaque paint and a small brush. Note the strong contrast created between the bright highlight area of the nose and the shadow of the eyes.

1. Draw up the outline of the head and features in black with a No 5 bristle brush. Block in areas of tone with Prussian blue and burnt sienna.

2. Mix warm flesh tones from red, yellow, black and white. Work over the face with patches of solid color. Lay in the background with greenish-greys.

6. Draw back into the features with black and lighten shadows with an overlay of yellow ochre. Lighten the background tone behind the head.

7. Once dry, put another thin red glaze over the flesh tones rubbing the paint in with a rag. Darken the background with a thick layer of black.

Finished picture · altering face · dark and light contrasts

Radical changes made during the painting process can often yield interesting results, especially if the original design is left only partly obscured. In this case, the artist chose to alter the face to correct anatomical features (<u>right</u>) and heighten compositional interest.

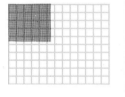

3. Highlight the face and hair with light pink and white and scumble a warm orange over the background to the left. Work loosely, laying broad, grainy marks.

4. Brush in dark tones in black defining the shape of the head and detailing features with a No 8 brush. Dry brush dark shadows across the flesh tones.

5. Lay a thin glaze of wet red paint over the whole face and heighten light tones with heavy dabs of pink and yellow.

8. Work over the background with hot reds and violet. Adjust the flesh tones with layers of broken color, blending the colors with a rag.

9. Rework the shapes in the face with fine black lines and dark shadows under the nose and behind the head. Block in strong white and light pink highlights.

10. Continue to model the form of the face and hair with light pink, yellow, and mauve tones. Dab in shadows with dark brown and violet.

ACRYLICS ARE time savers. While this painting could have been executed in oil, it would have taken much longer to complete. To achieve the changes shown, each stage would have to be thoroughly dry before alterations could be made. With acrylics, because of their fast drying time, the artist was able to work from start to finish without stopping and starting.

Examination of the first and last steps of the painting shows that, with the sole exception of the figure, the artist has almost completely re-arranged the picture. The changes were made largely for the sake of creating a more interesting composition. The original picture, while strong in its use of horizontals and verticals, was too complex and over-powered the figure. In removing the various squares and rectangles, the artist redirected the emphasis of the painting on to the figure. The addition of the bed and canvas on the same horizontal plane as the figure brings the viewer's eyes into the centre and, thus, concentrates them on the subject.

Materials

Surface
Stretched, primed canvas

Size
20in × 15in (50cm × 37cm)

Tools
No 4 flat bristle brush
Assorted palette knives
Soft pencil or charcoal sticks
Palette

Colors
Black	Chrome green
Burnt umber	Flake white
Cadmium yellow	Gold ochre
Cerulean blue	Prussian blue

Medium
Turpentine

Painting with knife and brush

Broad areas of this painting were described with thick paint and palette knives. Smaller detail areas were created with a No 2 brush and thinner washes of color.

1. With a soft pencil or willow charcoal, very lightly draw in the main horizontals and verticals of the compositon.

2. With a small rag, block in the background with a thin wash of cerulean blue. Do the same for the floor with cobalt blue and gold ochre.

3. Using a palette knife, mix a thick mixture of white and cerulean blue and cover the entire background and foreground areas.

4. Mix cerulean blue, a touch of black and white and block in the area around the floor with a palette knife. Add more blue and work into the background.

5. With a No 4 brush, describe the figure in black and white. Cover over the entire floor surface with cerulean blue and white on a palette knife .

6. Mix a light tone of grey, black, white and a touch of cerulean blue and cover the floor color. Lighten the background area with white and cerulean blue.

7. With a small brush and grey, put in the bed. Cover area directly behind in blue-grey tone using a knife. Put in flesh tone with ochre and white.

8. With a dark grey mixture made from cerulean blue, black and white, describe the shadow under the chair with a knife.

9. With white and terre verte, put in canvas to right of figure. Warm the flesh tones of the figure by glazing over with yellow ochre, umber, and linseed oil.

MANY ARTISTS will use acrylics for an underpainting and then finish off the work in oil paint. Note, however, that this process cannot be reversed, with an oil underpainting used for an acrylic painting, as a water-based paint will not adhere to an oil-based paint. This would also defeat the purpose of using an acrylic underpainting as the aim is to shorten the drying time and oils take much longer to dry than acrylics.

The painting develops as a series of steps in which the artist modelled the figure out of warm and cool tones, constantly watching their effect on one another and on the painting as a whole. Using a thin wash, a warm tone for the flesh would be put down and then overlaid with a cooler, lighter shade. Outlines and feature details would then be reinforced, and the process would begin again.

The warmth of the colors used in the figure are set off and heightened by the cool background. A similarly cool, light color has been used for highlight details in the face which link the sitter and the environment.

It is interesting to note that the various areas of the painting have been treated differently – the torso and background are not as highly developed as the head, for instance. This is effective in portraiture, since a generalized area around the sitter will draw the viewer's eyes to the face – the most important area.

Materials

Surface
Prepared canvas board

Size
18in × 24in (45cm × 60cm)

Tools
No 6 flat bristle brushes
No 4 sable round brush
Palette

Colors

Burnt sienna	Cobalt blue
Burnt umber	Pthalo crimson
Cadmium green	Pthalo violet
Cadmium red light	White
Cerulean blue	Yellow ochre

Medium
Water

1. Using thin wash and a No 6 brush, block in main color areas with pthalo crimson, burnt sienna, yellow ochre, white and cerulean blue.

2. With burnt umber and a No 4 brush, define dark areas draw in the features. Block in shadow areas behind head and with pure white put in light area.

3. Mix lighter flesh tone of yellow ochre and white and work over previous layer to emphasize highlights. Mix yellow ochre and red to create hair highlights.

4. With a No 6 brush, mix a pale tone of white and pthalo violet and block in the background with large strokes, blending the paint well into the surface.

5. When dry, work back over face, glazing in strong highlight areas with thin wash of white and water

6. Mix white, yellow ochre and a little red. With a No 4 brush, put in warm color areas of the face. Mix pthalo violet and white and rework background.

Blocking in hair

The dark shadow area in the hair is blocked in with black paint. This is used basically as an underpainting to be modified and toned down by later overpainting with warmer, lighter shades.

Watercolor

IN THIS PAINTING, thin, transparent layers of watercolor have been laid one on top of another giving the flesh a truly 'flesh-like' feeling and texture. Few other painting media are capable of this effect.

This painting exemplifies many of the more sophisticated ways in which watercolor may be used to create a strong but subtle portrait. The methods used require a steady hand, and familiarity with and confident use of the various watercolor techniques.

The flesh tones of the face, which, from a distance, merge into a continuous area of light and dark, were individually laid down and then blended with a clean, wet brush. Yellow and green were used to render the warm and cool tones of the flesh. The very dark details of the face were described in a strong burnt umber which contrasts with the pale flesh tone and emphasizes their importance.

Materials

Surface
Smooth board

Size
16in × 23in (40cm × 57.5cm)

Tools
Nos 00, 1 and 2 sable watercolor brushes
2B pencil
Colored pencils

Colors
Watercolor:

Burnt umber	Chrome green
Cadmium red	Ultramarine blue
Cadmium yellow	Yellow ochre

Colored pencils:
Grey
Red

Medium
Water

Working light to dark · shirt shadows · colored pencils

Watercolor is especially well-suited for portraiture. Because of the inherent transparency of the medium, it is important that the overall image has a strong composition. In this picture, the artist has surrounded the figure with almost empty space to draw the observer's eye into the figure.

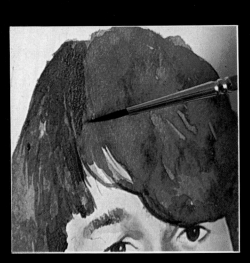

The entire painting progresses from light to dark. Here the artist is putting another wash of color over the hair to create a darker tone.

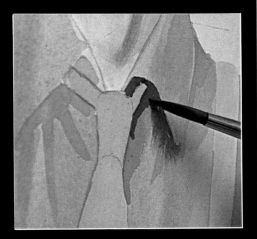

Using a strong blue and small sable brush, shadow areas are created in the shirt. Notice how the paint naturally bleeds into the damp surface, creating a gradated tone.

Once the paint surface is thoroughly dry, the artist works back into the face and detail areas with colored pencil, strengthening outlines and shadow areas with light hatching strokes.

1. Begin by putting in the mid and shadow tones with a thin wash of burnt sienna and green. With a small sable brush and pure umber, add eye details.

3. Apply a thin wash of yellow ochre over the face and work wet-in-wet with a light wash of green in the shadow area.

5. Darken hair color with burnt umber and a fine brush.

2. Continue with dark details of the eyes, nose and mouth. If the paint becomes too wet, blot with a tissue and then rework.

4. Block in the shirt with a thin wash of ultramarine blue. Carry yellow ochre tone into pants leaving white of paper for highlight areas.

6. With red pencil, work into the face with very light, diagonal strokes, heightening warm areas. With a grey pencil, strengthen horizontal lines of door.

37

A QUICK WATERCOLOR portrait may result in an interesting finished picture or may be used as reference for a larger work. This painting shows a lively impression of the overall form of face and figure, lightly modelled with color and tone.

The essence of the technique is to lay the color in watery pools which give the surface a loose, rippling texture. The painting must be allowed to dry frequently to get the full effect of overlaid washes and liquid shapes. It is important to keep the colors bright and true; you need to use plenty of clean water and rinse out the brushes thoroughly after each color application. Start by picking out small shapes of strong tone and color and develop the form in more detail as the painting progresses, drawing separate elements together to construct the entire image.

Since the painting is quite small you need only one brush to lay in the washes, and a finer point to draw up small linear details in the features. Make a brief pencil sketch to establish a guideline at the start but allow the painting to develop freely drawing over the pencil lines with the brush.

Materials

Surface
Stretched cartridge paper

Size
12in × 16in (30cm × 40cm)

Tools
Nos 3 and 7 sable watercolor brushes
Plate or palette

Colors

Black	Gamboge yellow
Burnt sienna	Scarlet lake
Burnt umber	Ultramarine blue
Cobalt blue	

Medium
Water

1. Work over the hair and face with wet pools of color – scarlet, yellow and burnt sienna – letting the tones blend. Drop light touches of cobalt blue into the shadows.

2. Block in thin patches of colour in the background and heavy washes of ultramarine to show the folds in the clothes.

3. Strengthen the color over the whole image, developing the structure of the forms. Keep the paint fluid and allow the colors to merge on the surface.

4. Model the face with heavy patches of red and brown, drawing in detail around the eyes with the point of a brush. Extend the background color.

5. Use mixtures of ultramarine and burnt umber to darken the shadows. Redefine the shapes in eyes and mouth.

6. Lay in a black wash across the background to bring the shape of the head forward. Add detail to the forms and strengthen the colors.

Using paper tone

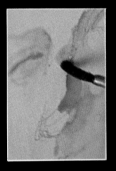

To create face details, the artist runs loose washes of color into one another leaving the paper tone to define highlights.

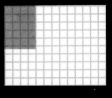

WATERCOLOR IS an excellent medium for painting children. It is delicate and subtle, with light flesh tones and soft shadows evolving gradually through layers of thin, pale washes applied over details.

When painting children, the temptation is often to make them look like small adults. For this reason, details of the pose which are characteristically childlike, such as the roundness of unformed features and smooth skin, must be captured exactly. It is usually easier to work from a photograph as lengthy sittings may be boring for a child. Take several photographs and choose the one which best suits the purpose, or use several in combination as reference.

The range of colors here is limited to shades of red, grey and brown. Blue was added to the browns and greys in the shadow areas to contrast with the overall warm tone of the colors. The image is drawn with the brush over a light pencil outline, first establishing the shapes and tones in the head and moving down to block in the entire body. Details in face and hair are drawn in fine lines with the point of the brush and then overlaid with washes of color. Dry-brush is used to create soft textures by loading a brush with dryish paint and, with the bristles spread between finger and thumb, drawing the brush across the paper to form light, broken strands of color.

Materials

__Surface__
Watercolor paper

__Size__
16in × 22.5in (40cm × 56cm)

__Tools__
No 3 round sable watercolor brush
Palette or plate

__Colors__
Black
Burnt sienna   Payne's grey
Burnt umber   Scarlet lake
Cobalt blue   Yellow ochre

__Medium__
Water

1. Work up detail around the eyes with light red, grey and burnt umber using a No 3 brush. Put in strands of hair.

2. Show soft shadows under the chin and mouth with light red and Payne's grey. Block in the body with a light wash of grey.

Using the same tone as for the shirt, made lighter by adding water, the artist puts in very pale shadow areas on the face.

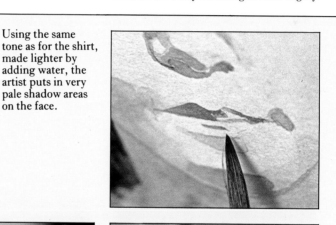

To create a dry-brush effect, dip a brush in paint and blot on a towel or rag. Press the brush hairs between thumb and finger to spread the hairs and brush on to the surface with light, feathering strokes using only the tips of the hairs.

3. Model the features more clearly with grey and brown washes. Lay in a strong black shadow to one side of the face.

4. Draw up the folds and patterning in the blouse with lines and washes of dark grey, drawing with the tip of the No 3 brush.

5. Work over the whole painting adding small touches of tone and color, elaborating details with the same brush.

Finished picture · facial shadows · using dry-brush

The full-faced centred portrait is perhaps the most direct way for the artist to present his subject. If the media and techniques used are handled carefully and thoughtfully, the overall effect can be both strong yet subtle.

THE PAINTING technique used here is loose and fluid and thus suited to the relaxed, informal attitude of the subject. This is basically a simple color study, as the forms are suggested in the brushwork rather than through accurate drawing and meticulous modelling. The figure is emphasized by the strong dark tones of clothes and hair and broad areas of black are enlivened with touches of vivid dark blue, violet and warm browns.

The whole composition is built up by laying in small local shapes and colors, gradually drawing them together into a coherent image. The vitality of this type of study depends upon working quickly, letting the eye travel across the subject to pick out color relationships, and translating them on to the paper with fluid and vigorous brushwork. Keep the brushes well loaded with paint so that each line and shape flows freely on to the paper and the liquid colors merge gently together.

Let the painting dry out completely from time to time so that subsequent color washes are fresh and sharp. If the painting is still wet the fine lines will spread and lose definition.

Small linear details such as the eyes and mouth should be drawn over a dry wash with the tip of a brush.

Materials

Surface
Stretched cartridge paper

Size
15in × 18in (38cm × 45cm)

Tools
HB pencil
Nos 3 and 7 round sable watercolor brushes
Plate or palette

Colors

Black	Scarlet lake
Burnt sienna	Ultramarine blue
Cadmium yellow	Violet
Prussian blue	

Medium
Water

1. Draw the basic shapes in the figure and background with an HB pencil. Wash in patches of strong wet color – black, burnt sienna, violet, Prussian blue and yellow.

2. Work into the flesh tones with washes of light red using a No 7 brush. Loosely apply colored shapes over the whole painting to indicate the forms.

3. Strengthen the blacks and draw into the pattern of the skirt with a No 3 brush. Bring together the background shapes with blocks of solid color.

4. Put in dark shadows on the face and arms with burnt umber and violet. Lay in light washes of blue and green across the background letting the colors run.

5. Work on the modelling of the figure with dark tones, defining the details of face and hands. Use muted tones in the background to draw the figure forward.

6. Continue to work on the figure gradually developing the tonal contrasts. Draw the features more finely with the point of the brush.

Finished picture · wet underpainting

The full length portrait presents the artist with a number of options and challenges and is often more difficult than the head-only variety. Included in the decisions to be made are where and how to place the figure, and how much of the background area to include.

In the initial stages, thin washes of color are laid down to describe shape and form. Note in the figure's hair how the paint has bled outward to create a natural outline.

Finished picture · wet underpainting

WHILE THIS painting may prove difficult to think of as a serious watercolor portrait, it expresses some of the most attractive attributes of the medium for the artist.

Despite its humorous aspect, the techniques and composition should not be overlooked. It is largely through the unique placement of the figure and the use of the clean, white space around it which forces the viewer's eye into the face of the subject. The strong darks of the hat and beard contrast boldly with the white of the paper making it impossible for the observer not to look directly into the face. This, coupled with the meticulous control of the medium and light, informal rendering of the shirt, serve to emphasize the focus of the painting.

Materials

Surface
Watercolor paper

Size
16in × 23in (40cm × 57.5cm)

Tools
2B pencil
No 4 sable watercolor brush
Palette or plate

Colors
Alizarin crimson
Black
Burnt sienna
Payne's grey

Medium
Water

1. With a No 4 brush, describe the hat and beard in Payne's grey. Keep the paint very wet and draw in outlines carefully, using only the tip of the brush.

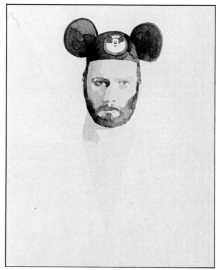

2. With same color, define the eyes, nose and mouth. Describe detail of hat in red.

3. Work over the face and neck with a darker wash of burnt umber and a touch of red to build up the picture.

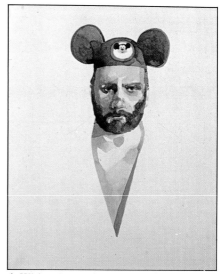

4. With a thin wash of Payne's grey, lay in shadow area of neck and chest.

5. Wet area of shirt with a clean brush and water. Very quickly lay down a wash of light Payne's grey, letting the tones run into the paper and one another.

6. While still wet, work back into the shirt with a thin wash of burnt umber, allowing drops to fall from the brush.

Blocking in color · tones and textures

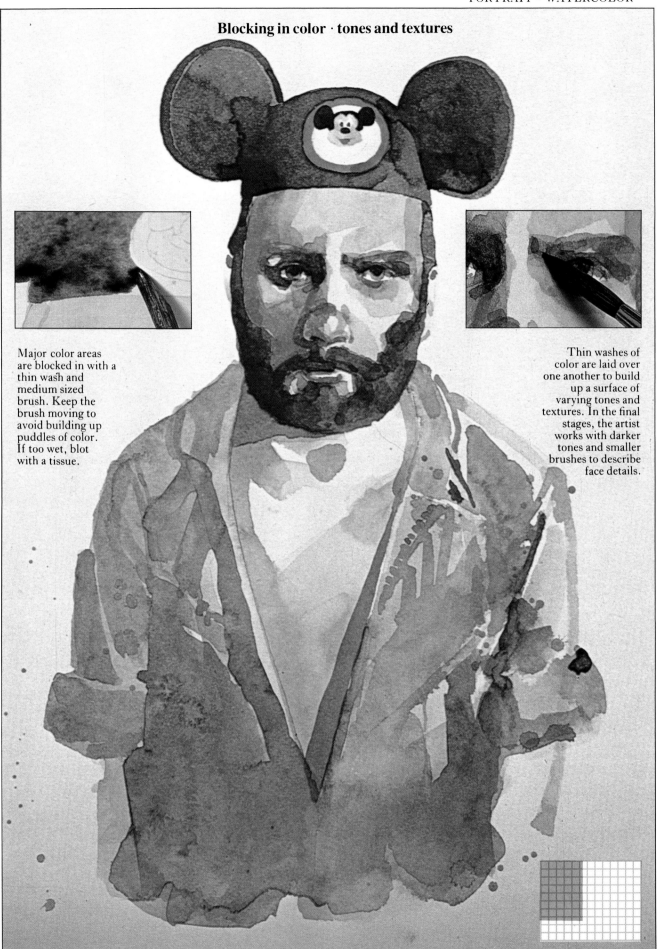

Major color areas are blocked in with a thin wash and medium sized brush. Keep the brush moving to avoid building up puddles of color. If too wet, blot with a tissue.

Thin washes of color are laid over one another to build up a surface of varying tones and textures. In the final stages, the artist works with darker tones and smaller brushes to describe face details.

45

Gouache

GOUACHE IS a convenient medium for doing quick color studies. It is cleaner to work with than oils and is also more opaque and matt than watercolors or acrylics. The colors are clear and intense. When mixed with white, they form a wide range of bright pastel tints suitable for the skin tones in a portrait. Because the paint is opaque you can work light over dark or vice versa, adjusting the tonal scale of the painting at any stage. The paint is reasonably stable when dry and thin washes of color can be laid over without damaging previous layers.

By studying the head in this painting carefully, the relationships between form and color become apparent. Work in small shapes of color, drawing with the brush to model curves and angles. A loose charcoal drawing is a helpful guideline at the start and can later be used to redefine outlines if the paint is not too thick. Adding black to make shadow areas may dull a color; shadows on the skin usually have a subtle cast of color such as green, blue or purple which can be used instead of black. Contrast these shadows with red and yellow within the lighter tones

Materials

Surface
Stretched cartridge paper

Size
16in × 20in (40cm × 50cm)

Tools
Medium willow charcoal
Nos 3 and 6 sable round brushes
Plate or palette

Colors

Alizarin crimson	Cobalt blue
Black	Flame red
Burnt sienna	Violet
Burnt umber	White
Cadmium yellow	Yellow ochre

Medium
Water

1. Draw the outline of head and shoulders with charcoal, indicating eyes, nose and mouth. Lay thin washes of red and brown to indicate shadows with a No. 6 brush.

2. Identify basic colors in the face and neck. Draw out contrasts by exaggerating the tones slightly, overlaying patches of each color to build up the form.

3. Draw into face with charcoal and paint in linear details with the point of a No 3 brush in dark brown. Work up the color in and around the features.

4. Alter the shape of the head and lay in dark tones of the hair. Paint the stripe pattern on the scarf in cobalt blue and strengthen the red of the jacket.

5. Develop the structure and colour of the face, drawing into the features with the No 3 brush and adding thick white and pink highlights with brown shadows in the flesh.

6. Block in the hair with a thin wash of yellow ochre and delineate separate strands with burnt umber. Reinforce the shapes of eyes and mouth with small color details.

46

Modelling with tone

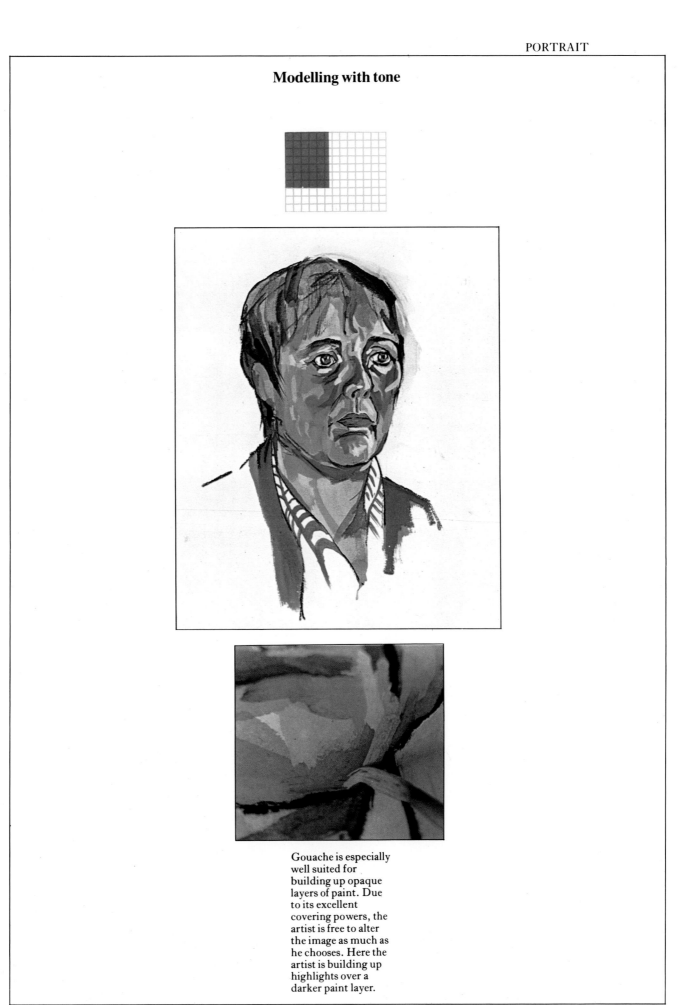

Gouache is especially
well suited for
building up opaque
layers of paint. Due
to its excellent
covering powers, the
artist is free to alter
the image as much as
he chooses. Here the
artist is building up
highlights over a
darker paint layer.

Pencil

TO CREATE a quick, informal portrait, any artist needs to be familiar with the chosen medium and techniques. Naturally, a sound knowledge of human anatomy is beneficial for all figure and portrait artists. Regardless of a person's distinguishing features, what lies beneath the surface – muscles, tendons, bones and cartilage – are the building blocks for all portrait and figure work. If the artist knows, for example, why an eye looks like it does – where it bulges and where it recedes – he will be that much closer to creating an accurate likeness.

This is especially true when doing a quick sketch, as the goal is to capture only the essential and outstanding characteristics of the model as quickly as possible. A labored and detailed drawing would allow the artist to study, correct, and change the drawing; but a quick sketch demands that the artist be able to accurately render the subject, since he will not be able to correct and revise.

Note, for example, how the artist has created the nose of the model and used directional lines to give form and depth. Through constant observation, studying and practice, the artist is able to quickly and effectively capture a likeness of the model.

Materials

Surface
Smooth, heavy weight drawing paper

Size
24in × 30in (60cm × 75cm)

Tools
2B and 4B drawing pencils
Eraser
Tissues or torchon
Fixative

1. With a 2B pencil, sketch in the general shape of the head. Position features in relation to one another, using very light strokes.

3. To bring the nose forward, crosshatch in shadow areas. Develop structure of face with light, widely spaced strokes. Refer to the subject to check the drawing.

5. Draw in the neck and shirt collar. Darken all detailed areas with contour strokes.

2. Begin to work into the shadow areas around the eyes with light crosshatching. Develop the hair with strokes which follow general contours.

4. With a 4B pencil, rework the shadow areas to darken tone. Work back into shadow areas with a putty eraser to erase highlights or lighten tones.

6. Blend in shadow area in neck with tissue or torchon. Put in shadow area outside of the face and blend. Erase back into highlights within the face.

Final details and crosshatching tones

Detailed areas of
the drawing are
developed in the
final stages. Note
the use of strokes
to develop strong
shadow areas.

THIS PICTURE is a good example of the effective use of colored pencils in portraiture, especially when combined with the color of the clean white surface.

Although the artist has used line to develop tonal areas, the method of drawing is similar to the classic oil painting technique of laying down colors one over another to 'mix' new colors. This requires a confident use of color, as once put down, colored pencils are not easily erased. This, combined with subtle or strongly directed strokes which follow or exaggerate the planes of the figure, creates a powerful image.

An interesting feature of the composition is the use of the white paper within the figure to describe the face, hands, and hair highlights. In the model's left hand, one simple line is all that is needed to separate the figure from its environment. The nearly bare areas of the face and hands are heightened by the surrounding dark area, which, in turn, plays off against the white of the paper.

Materials

<u>Surface</u>
White drawing paper

<u>Size</u>
12in × 16in (30cm × 40cm)

<u>Colors</u>

Dark red	Raw umber
Light green	Ultramarine blue
Magenta	Yellow ochre

Initial color areas · dark details

In the final stages of drawing, the artist reworks dark detail areas with a strong blue pencil.

The outlines of the figure are first sketched in with a warm brown. The artist then blocks in shadow areas with a cool blue. Here he is working back into the face with light strokes of orange to begin to build up flesh tones. Note the use of loose strokes.

1. Sketch in the outline of the face in raw umber. Use ultramarine blue for shadows and hair and very light strokes of the same color in the blouse.

2. With pale green, begin to define shadow areas of the face with very light hatching and crosshatching. With dark blue, put in the eye details.

3. With red and yellow, put in loose strokes to define hair tone. Strengthen outlines of face with ultramarine blue. Put in dark shadow area to right of face

4. Work into the hair with directional strokes of red. Overlay light strokes of blue and red in the blouse with loose, scratching strokes.

5. Overlay magenta area with red. Create stronger shadow areas with ultramarine blue.

6. Work back into hair with burnt umber. Use pale green to put in highlights in the cup.

51

THIS DRAWING RELIES largely on the use of loose, flowing lines and areas of tone to create the image. The drawing was executed rapidly with just essential shapes and tones used to describe the sitter. The emphasis of the drawing is on the face and hands, making the figure a self-contained, stable unit.

A high contrast is developed in the face of the model which, with the use of the pure white paper and very dark details, focuses the viewer's attention on the head area. The relaxed line work and shading within the torso lend the figure both weight and movement. While solid and stable, the impression is that the figure could get up or change his position at any moment. The value of using a quick, informal approach to drawings of this type becomes evident especially when the pose is difficult or uncomfortable for the model and he or she is apt to move or tire easily.

Materials

Surface
Smooth white drawing paper

Size
15in × 16.5in (37.5cm × 41cm)

Tools
2B and 4B drawing pencils
Putty eraser
Fixative
Tissues

1. Sketch in the outlines of the figure very loosely with a 2B pencil. Rough in the eyes, nose, and mouth.

2. With quick, light, directional strokes, put the shadow areas of the hair and figure into the drawing.

3. Work back into the head of the figure with a 4B pencil strengthening dark areas. With the same, outline shoulder and neck.

4. With a 2B pencil work back into the shadow areas. Redefine leg and feet outlines as necessary.

5. With the 4B pencil, go over the lower half of torso with quick, light strokes building up shadow tones. Work back into the head to heighten darks.

6. With the 2B pencil, define fingers and hands. Put in shadow area beneath them.

Using tone and stroke to develop the figure

The shadow areas on the face are developed with diagonal strokes of soft grey tone. Both the tone of the pencil and the direction of the strokes help give the impression of depth and form.

Pastel

THERE IS A long history of pastel portrait drawing and some of these drawings, with their finished surface of subtly blended color, are nearly indistinguishable from an oil painting. In fact, the term 'pastel painting' has become as common as 'pastel drawing'. While the early pastellists most likely spent as much time on their work as a painter would on an elaborate portrait, contemporary artists have developed techniques of drawing which are flexible and less time-consuming than these early drawing methods.

The basic structure of this drawing is built upon woven lines and hatched blocks of tone using a limited range of colour. Once the fundamental shapes and tones are established, the subject is rendered with layers of bright color.

Pastel is powdery and difficult to work with if the surface becomes too densely covered. Thus, it is worthwhile to spray the drawing with fixative frequently to keep the color fresh and stable.

Materials

Surface
Beige pastel paper

Size
25in × 18in (62.5cm × 45cm)

Tools
Soft, large brush for blending
Pastles
Putty eraser
Fixative

Colors
Apple green   Scarlet
Black   Ultramarine blue
Light blue   Venetian red
Pink   White
Prussian blue   Yellow

1. Draw up the basic shapes of the image in Prussian blue, sketching in rough outlines and a brief indication of tones.

3. Refine details of the features with strong lines of dark blue and flesh out the face with solid blocks of white and red.

5. Block in light tones in the face with pink and pale blue. Lay in broad areas of dark tone with black and Prussian blue, working out from the figure.

7. Lay in dark background tones to emphasize the form of the figure. Overlay and blend the colors to mix the tones, working over the whole image.

2. Build up the linear and tonal structure with Venetian red, developing the loose modelling of the forms. Strengthen the drawing with fine black lines.

4. Spray the work with fixative and let it dry. Draw into the figure with blue and black correcting the outlines and adding extra details in line and tone.

6. Develop the intensity of color, using strong, bright hues to lift the overall tone. Link vivid yellow highlights on the face with the same color in the background.

8. Bring out the form with strong white highlights. Apply the pastel thickly and blend the color softly with a dry brush. Strengthen light tones in the background.

Strengthening background and face with black

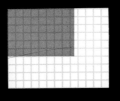

Once general shadow and highlight areas have been blocked in, the artist works back into the picture with a black pastel to develop facial details. Here he is outlining the shape of the glasses.

With a black pastel, the artist darkens the shadow area beside the face. This has the effect of forcing the flesh tones of the face to stand out in bold relief.

THERE ARE good reasons for the fact that many pastel artists prefer to work on tinted paper. In this case, the flesh-toned paper has been used as part of the figure. As well as being a solid, neutral tone, it works to emphasize the strong colours used in the face and dress.

A minimum of blending has been used thus the technique of overlaying colors may be clearly seen. The hands reveal how the artist has used directional strokes of pure color to give them form and tone; throughout the figure the artist has changed the direction of the strokes to describe planes within the face and hands.

Materials

Surface
Pumpkin coloured pastel paper

Size
22in × 30in (55cm × 75cm)

Tools
Tissues or rags
Large, soft brush for blending
Fixative

Colors
Light grey
Dark grey
Black
White

1. Roughly describe the dark areas of the head and torso with loose strokes.

2. Put in hair highlights and eye details. With white, put in strong face highlights and strengthen outlines.

3. Fill in hair area describing shadow and highlights. Rough in chair and flower and draw in the hands.

4. Develop the shadow areas of the hands. If a part of the drawing proves difficult, use the rest of the page to do a detailed study.

5. Block in the lighter area of the chair. Work into shadow areas and blend and lay in the shadow areas in the dress.

6. Roughly describe the dress pattern with a mixture of tones.

Overlaying light tones · doing a detailed study

Here the artist overlays very dark shadow areas in the hair with a lighter, softer shade of brown.

If a part of the drawing proves difficult, a study can be done elsewhere on the page which can later be cropped from the finished picture.

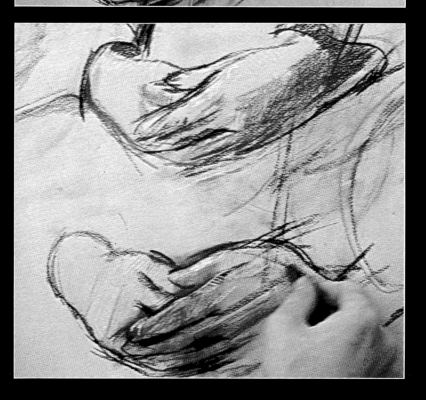

IN CAPTURING THE character of a subject, a quick sketch is often more successful than a carefully worked painting. The loose, vibrant colors of pastels are particularly suited for quick sketches using a vigorous, calligraphic style, as shape and texture can be shown through the activity of the color rather than the meticulous delineation of forms.

In this drawing, pastel strokes are multidirectional and the colors warm and bright, giving an impression of a fleeting image; the model is frozen in a split second of time, not carefully posed for a long sitting. This is a quality which photographers often capture, and thus photographs are often a good source of reference material for this type of portrait.

Tonal contrasts are skillfully manipulated with black used sparingly for dark tones and outlines. Facial shadows are created with mauve and a vivid dark red, and thick white highlights give an impression of light across the face. The movement and texture of the hair is represented by heavily scribbled strokes of bright orange.

Materials

<u>Surface</u>
Blue-grey pastel paper

<u>Size</u>
11in × 15in (27.5cm × 37.5cm)

<u>Tools</u>
Fixative

<u>Colors</u>

Black	Pink
Burnt sienna	Ultramarine blue
Mauve	White
Orange	Yellow

Blending preliminary tones · highlighting the face

After the outlines of the head are sketched in, the artist lays in very thin strokes of warm and cool tones, blending them with his fingers.

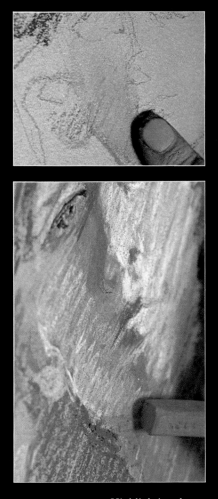

Highlighting the face with strong warm tones. Note how the artist has used strokes of pure color in the shadow areas and how the warm oranges and pinks mix with the cool, tinted paper.

1. Sketch in the outline of the figure in burnt sienna. Work into the face with lines of bright orange, ultramarine and pink against dark shadows in the hair.

3. Accentuate the shapes in the face with fine black lines and patches of strong colour. Heighten light tones with pink and mauve against warm dark red shadows.

5. Outline the hand and arm with black and block in dark flesh tones with orange and mauve. Lay in a dark blue background tone.

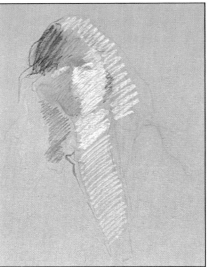

2. Hatch in light tones down one side of the figure with broad, grainy strokes of white. Move across the whole figure putting in orange, yellow and blue.

4. Build up the light colour in the face and work over the hair with heavy strokes of black, white and orange.

6. Draw vigorously into all the shapes with strong color, developing the tones and texture and highlighting the face and hand.

Pen and ink

A PROFILE CAN be as successful in capturing a person's likeness as the traditional full-faced portrait because it clearly shows the contours of the individual's features. In this painting, the structure of the form is broken into a pattern of shapes by extremes of light and shadow. A strong image is constructed by using the basic techniques of hatching and stippling. The drawing uses high tonal contrasts, but note that there are no solid black areas; the darkest tones consist of layers of dense crosshatching built up in patterns of parallel lines. Details of texture and shadow in the face are stippled with the point of the nib. The vigorous activity in the drawing is offset by broad patches of plain white paper indicating the fall of light over the form.

Observe the subject carefully as you work, moving the pen swiftly over the paper. Pen strokes should be loose and lively or the result can all too easily look stiff and studied.

Materials

Surface
White cartridge paper

Size
10in × 11.5in (25cm × 29cm)

Tools
HB pencil
Dip pen with medium nib

Colors
Black waterproof India ink

1. Hatch in a dark tone down one side of the head to throw the profile into relief. Continue to build up detail in the face.

2. Work on shadows inside the shape of the head with fine parallel lines slanted across the paper. Work outwards into the background in the same way.

3. Broaden out the shadows and crosshatch areas of the background behind the head to darken the tones.

4. Vary the tones in the background gradually covering more of the paper. Work into the head and clothes with small, detailed patterns.

5. Draw in patches of dark tone to show folds in the clothing. Define the hairline and shape of the ear with crosshatching.

6. Work over the whole image intensifying the tones with hatching and stippling. Develop a high contrast of light and dark down the face and body.

Using paper to model the face

The initial pencil sketch of the head is used only as a reference for developing shadow and highlight areas. Note in particular how the shadows within the face and in the background create the profile of the head.